ALF® SOUNDS OFF!

Written by Richard J Schellbach
Illustrated by Dick Codor

CHECKERBOARD PRESS ▨ NEW YORK

® © 1987 Alien Productions. All Rights Reserved.

Published by Checkerboard Press, a division of Macmillan, Inc.
CHECKERBOARD PRESS and colophon are trademarks of Macmillan, Inc.

ISBN: 0-02-688557-3

Designed by Bob Feldgus

10 9 8 7 6 5 4 3 2 1

Standing in the store aisle looking for a quick chuckle before you buy the stuff you came for? Well, stop peeking! Trust me . . . it's a funny book. (Would I lie?) So, come on, fork out the cash. I'd buy your book if you had one!

Ha, caught ya! I told you it was funny... so funny that you're peeking at another page! Come on, buy the thing and quit embarrassing yourself. You don't want all the people that are watching you to think you're cheap.

Words I Just Don't Understand...

RACKETEER:
I was really embarrassed to find out this had nothing to do with Annette Funicello playing tennis.

RECYCLE:
Isn't that when you ride your bike on the same route two days in a row?

RUTHLESS:
So sue me! I thought it meant Dr. Ruth's show got cancelled.

ALF TALKS ABOUT THE TUBE...

Why are all of the agricultural shows on at 5:30 in the morning, when the farmers are already outside working?

An alien can learn a lot from watching TV. For example, I never knew that before 1953 this entire planet was in black and white.

My favorite show is "Gilligan's Island." But how come all five passengers packed so many clothes for a three-hour tour?

If I've learned anything from watching TV, it's this: Those who can, act; those who can't, host game shows.

ALF On Death...

If you really can't take it with you, why does your life insurance policy only pay off *after* you're dead?

I've heard that on Earth, traffic accidents kill a lot of people. On Melmac, the biggest cause of accidental death was inhaling next to a talent agent.

I guess I'd attribute my long life to the fact that I haven't died yet.

ALF's Uncle Goomer...

My uncle Goomer was a brilliant inventor. I remember when I was just 116, he crossed a pigeon with peanut butter and got a bird that stuck to the roof of his house.

Sixteen years ago, Uncle Goomer got an Icky. No, it's not a disease . . . it's an award. He got it for being the host of Melmac's shortest-running game show, "Bowling for Lard."

Uncle Goomer's acting career ended when his voice changed and left him sounding like William F. Buckley.

ALF on living...

I finally figured out the difference between apartment living and owning your own home. If you live in an apartment, you have to pay to take a ride in the clothes dryer.

If Willie hates to mow the lawn so much, how come he waters it so often?

Why do humans spend twice as much money planting a garden as they save by growing their own food?

ALF ON FOOD...

It took me three months to realize that when the whipped cream can says "Shake well before using," they mean the can, not me.

I wish cats really did have nine lives. I love leftovers.

My idea of a balanced meal? As much food as I can carry in both hands without dropping it.

ALF on transportation

Willie told me that, in the sixties and seventies, all cars were named after animals. I'm surprised no one came up with a car called "The Gopher," for people who like to run their cars into the ground.

Why do earth cars have so many different gears? On Melmac we only had three: fast, really fast, and yikes, we're going to die!

Lynn was saying that, in high school, you have to take Driver's Ed. What I want to know is, who's Ed and where do you take him?

Melmacian riddles...

Q: What's green, moldy and covered with meat?
A: Stan, the barber.

Q: How many Melmacians does it take to screw in a lightbulb?
A: One. Why would it take any more than that?

Q: What do you get if you cross a fungle with a cat?
A: EEEW! How could you even consider that? Talk about kinky!

Q: What can you use a broken glazbarr for?
A: A paperweight. Ha!

All about Lynn...

I caught a peek at Lynn's new boyfriend, Melvin. Yikes! Now I know why some animals eat their young.

I'm serious about Melvin. The boy is hideous. I didn't think humans dated out of their species.

And they say talk is cheap. I can't wait to see the phone bills after Melvin leaves for college next month.

In the backyard...

Yesterday I saw Willie cooking on a grill in the backyard. He called it "barbecuing". On Melmac we did the same thing... but we called it "thinning the cat population."

Willie was in the backyard last week and he said he was "spraying for bugs." I thought we had enough bugs *before* he sprayed.

ALF on the English Language...

Earthlings say, "To err is human." I guess that's why I never make mistakes. Melmacians are perfect.

Earth mothers say the weirdest things. My favorite has to be, "Close your mouth and eat your dinner." Does that make sense to you?

And why do earthlings use terms like *jumbo shrimp* and *plastic glasses?* And when two planes almost collide they call it a *near miss.* That's a *near hit* in my book. (And let's face it—this *is* my book. Ha!)

Last week, Brian told me that he wanted to be the first kid to break the sound barrier. We took the engine out of my spaceship, remodeled it and strapped it onto his bike. He became the first kid to break the wall of the garage.

Earth children don't know how to live. I can't even get Brian to try my peanut butter and Spam pudding. Kids!

Am I brilliant? Yesterday I talked Brian into helping me staple the leaves on all of the trees in the backyard so we won't have to do any raking this fall.

More Words I Don't Understand...

PARADOX:
Call me stupid! I thought it was an abbreviation for two doctors.

RESIGN:
Isn't that what you do if your pen doesn't work the first time?

STEREOTYPE:
Brian told me it was two people typing at the same time! He was kidding, right?

I'm confused...

How many times have you heard someone ask for the "good scissors"? I'm confused. Why would anybody keep bad scissors lying around?

I learned something yesterday that really threw me. Why is it that a bottle of light beer weighs the same as a bottle of the regular stuff?

Who's the idiot who came up with setting your clocks ahead one hour in the spring when you're going to take the hour back in the fall? It all evens out at the end of the year, anyway!

ALF on cats...

I love cats. Especially with an order of fries.

Earth people say that cats are independent. Personally, I prefer them in-de-oven.

Since I've landed on earth, I haven't eaten a single cat. They've all been married.

On Dieting...

I hate being on this stupid diet. It messes up my television viewing. I was going to watch "Cat on a Hot Tin Roof" tonight, but I'm afraid it will only make me hungry.

Kate caught me trying to steal a chocolate chip cookie. I guess I shouldn't be surprised that she nabbed me . . . it was in her mouth at the time.

As my wise old uncle used to say, "Dieting is hard. Calling out for pizza is easy."

ALF on Manners...

From now on, I'm going to try not to talk with my mouth full. Of course, that would be a vow of silence, wouldn't it?

If it's acceptable to pick one's teeth after one eats, why is your nose off limits after a sneeze?

If you belch after a meal in Japan, it's considered a compliment. In America, it's considered rude. I guess that gives me a semi-excuse to let one rip after sushi.

Why is it that earthlings put their dirty clothes into a basket, take them out, wash them in a washing machine, then throw the clean clothes back into the same basket?

And another thing . . . why do earthlings take a shower to get clean, then dry themselves off with a towel they've been using for days?

And speaking of being clean, why is it that fruit that is ripe smells good, but earthlings that are "ripe" smell bad?

More Earth words I don't understand...

EXPOUND:
The weight you lost.

SUPERIMPOSE:
When you stay at a party after everyone else has left.

Come on, I don't speak Chinese either! I'm only nonhuman.

ALF ON MOVIES...

Zombie movies have done wonders for my ego. When I see things crawl out of the grave after 50 years, I realize I look darn good for 229.

How come in old movies no one ever finishes the line, "Why, I oughtta . . ."?

SPORTS AND MORE SPORTS

I can understand Yankees, Tigers, Angels, Giants and even Dodgers... but could somebody please tell me what a Met is?

With all those slobs dribbling on the basketball court, how come the floor's not slippery?

Before the fifties, was color commentating done in black and white?

■ ■ ■ ■ ■ ■ ■ ■ ■ ■ ■ ■ ■ ■ ■ ■ ■

What Earthlings do in the name of health...

They say swimming is a good way to exercise. Funny, I always thought it was a way to avoid drowning.

Now the latest diet craze is eating seaweed. Gimme a break! If the fish won't eat it, why should I?

Ever since Kate and Willie switched to decaffeinated coffee, they can't stay awake long enough to finish drinking it.

MORE TALK ABOUT THE TUBE...

I've heard people say that soap operas are addictive. They haven't phased me... I've been watching every day for a year.

By the way... how can something called a "soap" be so dirty?

Earth game shows aren't challenging enough. On Melmac, if you lose, people come to your house and take your furniture away.

SCHOOL TALK...

On Melmac, we didn't get homework. It might have been because we went to school *24* hours a day.

We also had the three R's: reading, 'riting and rodent control. (By the way, have you guys figured out that arithmetic doesn't start with the letter *R*?)

Obviously, our biology classes were different from yours. And we never quite got to the dissection stage . . . Arty Frizzborn kept eating our specimens.

AMERICA, AMERICA...

Why does the United States have so many cultural differences? On the East Coast, people "eat" lunch . . . on the West Coast, they "do" lunch. (Does "doing" too much make you as sick as "eating" too much does?)

Obviously, there is life on other planets. But why, when they visit Earth, do they usually land on a farm in Bakersfield and abduct people with two first names?

If baseball is called "America's Favorite Pastime," why does America have more babies than baseballs?

ALF ON CHORES...

As far as I'm concerned, the Tanners and I split the housekeeping right down the middle. I keep the house dirty . . . they try to keep it clean.

Last week, I decided to help Willie by cleaning the pool. He told me that next time I should use a brush. By the way, the blisters on my tongue are finally starting to clear up.

I wish the Tanners would label the bottles under the bathroom sink. Yesterday I cleaned the toilet seat with Super Glue. ("Hang in there, Willie! The fire department's on the way!")

■ ■ ■ ■ ■ ■ ■ ■ ■

MORE ON MOVIES ...
(or should it be "moron movies"?)

Why do Earth's most talented filmmakers usually get a Life Achievement Award after they're dead? Is that the only way to shorten the acceptance speech?

I'm really starting to get into horror movies. So far, my favorites are *Yawn of the Dead* (1978's sleeper) and *Maximum Overbite* (just when you thought it was safe to go back to the dentist . . .).

I heard that Vanna White is going to star in the remake of *The Vowel and the Pussycat.*

ALF's definitions...

COUCH POTATOES:
Vegetables that can be grown in the living room.

STONE-BLIND:
Someone who constantly trips over rocks.

BISEXUAL:
A deviate on two wheels.

Some general comments...

Watching soap operas has taught me something important... the quickest way to get out of the hospital is to tell the doctor that you lied about having medical insurance.

Don't worry about looking your true age. On Melmac, trying to look younger was hazardous to one's health. Once, my mother tried to dye her hair. She almost drowned.

I can't seem to figure out what it is that politicians do. Fortunately for them, neither can most of the people who vote!

So, was it good for you too? Did you laugh? Did this book make you forget the fact that your toilet overflowed so much that the plumber had to wear scuba gear to fix it . . . or that this morning your kids shaved the dog and painted him orange? Well, don't worry about those things. I'm sure something else happened while you were reading this. Ha! Just kidding. I kill me.

ALFectionately,

ALF